To   V......

my very best

michael Ed...

RUNAWAYS

POWELL KIMBELL

authorHOUSE®

AuthorHouse™
1663 Liberty Drive
Bloomington, IN 47403
www.authorhouse.com
Phone: 1 (800) 839-8640

Published by AuthorHouse 05/29/2019

ISBN: 978-1-7283-1369-6 (sc)
ISBN: 978-1-7283-1368-9 (e)

RUNAWAYS

Thomas says this is a story that needs to be told. No one would believe it, he says. Perhaps he is right. It's the story of two brothers, orphaned at ages two and four, moving from a desperate situation into a more desperate one. It is true, embellished only by time and the vagaries of memory. It is my story, our story, and ultimately, a timeless story.

THE RIVER

Looking down at that muddy water - looks like liquid mud. Roiling, boiling, fast moving, maybe swallow a man whole, never to be seen again. I don't know if this is the kind of river Huck Finn and Jim floated down in their story. They escaped on their river, and I am escaping on mine. Looks like this river can carry away two orphan brothers, eight and ten years old. Muddy river here, can hold us, carry us away; keep us away from all those demons of our present and past. So full of the faith and confidence in this muddy river, we jump in. Thomas is in the river, I'm in; it's time to float, float us away. We're ready, been ready, and so is the river. Hope nothing in this river eats us: giant catfish, alligator gar, and snapping turtles big as a car that can swallow a kid whole. Maybe other things here too, we don't know about yet. We left a dangerous world we know for one we don't know. Our experience of the outdoors and this river is the one we are learning right now.

The muddy current holds us up, we float past high mud embankments, and low shoals on the opposite side. There are no people, no bridges, no roads, and no boats. We float in isolated splendor. The sun rises to midday heat in a cloudless sky. The river is a living thing, itself filled with life. A turtle basks on a log on a bank, a fin breaks the brown surface, and birds live in the tangled overgrowth. Swarms of gnats, a dragonfly above moving water. Something unseen escapes the tangle at our approach. A hawk floats in a blue haze of cloudless sky. We float in a primitive solitude and time floats with us. Time, space, and this river that moves us, are our friends, our only friends. We are carried away, and away is our only goal. Thomas wonders how fast we are moving away. So we look at the current, guess it at three to five mph, so several hours may give us ten to fifteen miles of distance, for free. Our minds seem to see, measure, taste this new freedom, and it tastes good, a taste neither of us remember. A taste of sun, sky, river, earth. It speaks to us, and we hear. Our eyes open, and we understand, and float. We acquire a large dead log on the riverbank, float it with some effort, and climb on top. The log is top heavy with us on it, and it rolls us until we are upside down. We repeat this process innumerable times; always with the same result. This log raft would not have served Huck Finn, and it does not serve us. With some reluctance, we abandon our ship, resolving to find a better one; one that does not dunk us upside down every time we climb aboard.

We have been on the river for the afternoon. We think our drift has taken us ten, maybe fifteen miles outside of the city. It is far enough, remote enough to improve our chances of not being seen, or found. For the moment, we are unseen and vanished, for a full day and night. We are dirty, wet, tired, hungry, but we are free and alive. That is enough. There is no home or refuge behind us. We belonged to adoptive parents, both alcoholics, who visit us with unrelenting terror and fear. There are lulls in the ebb and flow of physical and emotional violence, but the pattern is the same. We believe they desire our destruction. And plan on doing so when they tire of tormenting us. We live in a home, unloved and unlovable. The mold is cast. We were given to them by other Big People whom we did not know. Searching for a home, a place we know, a place that knew us, we found this river. It immerses us, embraces us, and baptizes us in its muddy current, it whispers to us. It knows secrets that we do not. We were orphans; it welcomed us with its earthen banks and muddy water. Perhaps we were born here; in this muddy river and just now finding our way back home. The sky blazes overhead in a hot Oklahoma summer.

A roofline over the high embankment suggests a house. We scramble up the high embankment, through a jungle of tall overgrowth.

3

A grey, abandoned farmhouse greets us. We had imagined this, and here it is in decaying splendor. It hasn't been lived in for ten years or longer. There are no windows or doors or paint. The roof is still there, with walls, a floor, and a front porch. All suggestion of prior habitation is gone, nothing remains of creature comfort. But it is our 'new' home and it looks like paradise. A single lane dirt road graces the front yard, surrounded by vistas of unending corn fields. The corn towers to a regal ten feet overhead, in late summer. In the bloom of childhood innocence, naiveté; we do not consider harvesting and eating the corn. In the urgency of departure, we brought neither clothes, nor food, blankets, matches, or water. The earth would clothe and feed us, as it always had. In the past, eating was ritualized to specific times of the day. Food was there, and we ate. Here, we had to go out and find food (kill it?) In early discussion of how we would eat, Thomas proposed that we could shoot an occasional chicken with our bow and arrow. And while that makes no more sense now than it did then, his answer was at least an answer to an important question of our survival. And if we both had considerable experience at survival by age eight and ten, that experience did not include shooting chickens with a bow and arrow for food. Thomas suggests walking the dirt road, to see if it leads to a store. He wanted to go alone, as police may be looking for two young boys together. Off he goes, under my wistful gaze, disappearing into the tall green corn. He's back in several hours carrying candy bars, crackers, and a bag of white rice. It is evening and I am beyond ravenous. I ask Thomas if he is hungry, and he is not. Mysterious, until I consider he was likely eating all the way back. I asked him how we were going to eat white rice. He agreed we would need a fire, a pot, water, none of which we had. He did pass a small farmhouse on his way, where we could at least find water- another day perhaps. We had been gone now for twenty-four hours, a full day. Piled up straw in the corner of the bare living room invited rest, until ticks emerged, chasing us to hard flooring. Night was cold without blankets on hard ground, but we were full, ours was a sleep of exhaustion. The next day: the farmhouse.

THE FARMHOUSE

The concept of provisioning ourselves for a trip, any trip, was a new concept. As was the trip itself. So we found ourselves in a remote, isolated place without even the very basics, like matches, food and water. And then there were clothes, bedding, light, none of which we had. Our wet, muddy clothes from the river dried on us; the river claimed Thomas' shoes and the bow and arrows, as its toll for passage. I had wanted to bring my butterfly collection, but Thomas convinced me of the clear logic of doing otherwise. Our resources included the abandoned house we were in, the farmhouse Thomas had seen, and the store. As children, we hope for the kindness of strangers. We can at least get water, if nothing else, at the farmhouse.

The farmhouse appears less than a mile up the one-lane dirt road, to our left. A well fifty yards to the left of the house, in a plowed field, offers water. We walked up to the well; it appeared to be working, and clean. No containers. We approach the farmhouse. No sound comes from it; no dogs, people, no farm animals of any kind are around. The house itself is weathered, but clean and well-kept. We knock on the door. No answer. The door is unlocked; we open it with great trepidation. Our "Hello!" echoes around a vacant house. The gears shift in both our brains: find food. The house is small but cozy, nothing is out of place. Whoever lived here (perhaps a local Indian tribe member, Pawnee or Cherokee) took care of this house. We continue our urgent search for food. The kitchen is sparse, neat, and the cabinets contain a minimal stock of food. We get peanut butter, cereal, various canned foods, a can opener, spoons, a jar for water. Walking away with our booty, we notice our clear foot prints in the plowed ground coming from the well. Whoever lived here will also see those foot prints, and we both know in that instant our fates are sealed. The price of food. We put the thought out of mind, as we make our way back to our vacant house, and celebrate having food. Hope itself is renewed. Days were flowing by now, three days, and we are here, and alive. No bosses here. No one chasing us. We are still vanished from sight of the other world we fled. Perhaps this will be the start of our new life. It's been a big day for us. We sleep.

THE CAR

Morning finds us awake but groggy. Breakfast is dry cereal, water, peanut butter. It feels strange not being hungry, as though food had somehow upset a certain equilibrium, a delicate and precarious balance that we had acquired by art, instinct, and accident. Our stomachs were full, but uneasiness seemed to hang in the air. We view our space, a dusty farmhouse, surrounded by unending vistas of green corn as far as the eye could see. Corn, green corn, ten feet tall occupies the center of creation. The full sun is playing cloud shadows over vast green fields, all alive, all growing with a vibrancy of summer. The color of passion is green. My eyes cannot take it all in. At that moment, a black car appears on our dirt road, emerging from tall corn fields on the left, moving slowly directly in front of us, and vanishing out of sight to our right. Four to five men are in the car: they see us, we see them.

Time freezes, shrinks in upon itself. We are frozen. Our muscles tense to flee the opposite way, back through the overgrowth and into the river. Our only escape.

We breathe, and consider. There are no cars here, no traffic, no people; no nothing. Only us. This is the only car, the only people we have seen in three days. The men had a predatory look, as the car slowly drove by and vanished from view. It did not come back. Foreboding consumes us.

We are torn between waiting to see what happens and getting back into the river and putting distance between this place and us. We decide to wait to see if the car comes back, since many of these dirt roads dead end.

We wait, hovering on the edge of flight. All our instincts scream that this is wrong, this is true peril. We wait for the mysterious black car. We wait for synaptic flight to the river. We wait. Night falls.

We sleep.

THE CAPTURE

The quiet morning explodes as the black car moves out fast from the corn fields on our left. It could be a replay from yesterday, except it's not. It is sitting now in front of us, in an instant, all four doors fly open and men in dark clothes launch themselves out with true purpose. We glance at our meager possessions, there is no time. These men are coming real fast, right at us, right now.

Thomas and I peel off the opposite side of the porch, past tall weeds, into a clearing. We are in a dead sprint across the clear, grassy area. Tall overgrowth and River beyond scream; RUN! We run, as fast as legs can move, we run.

We are midway to safety of the river when a mounted man on horseback, with lariat, gallops from our left, to block our escape. He and the horse move as a single unit, with speed, precision, purpose. He is swinging his lariat, and we are surrendered, all in an instant. The men in the black car surround us; put us in the back seat with a man on either side. It is over. Our past has caught us, captured us.

Back at the City Police Station, a teenager sweeping up, a trustee, smirks as we emerge from the car. I look down at myself, and I am filthy. No shower for five days. He wears his smirk just like his clean, pressed white uniform. A sergeant in plain clothes, separates us, leads me into a small interview room, with a small white table and two brown wooden chairs. I am relieved he is not mad. He asks me about the farmhouse, if we were there, what we did. I told him we took food, water, matches, and a can opener. He asks if we took a watch. I say no. We were there for food, not a watch. He asks me how I feel about taking a can of government-provided peanut butter, given to the needy. I was hungry, I tell him. Your mother is coming to get you both, he tells me. She sure is, I think.

The world has recaptured its small fugitives. The trustee with the broom and white pressed uniform is still smirking as Thomas and I leave the police station. Our mother picks us up in the family Buick, we are captives again as we surrender to uncertainty, dread, molten fear. But Life is rarely as we script it. The promised beating we were expecting never came. Instead, she feeds us scrambled eggs, bacon, toast. Which felt like manna from Heaven, such was our hunger. Her actions and words had an unfamiliar, guarded quality. The beating I was promised and which prompted my flight never came during those days. The beating promised earlier to me came as a consequence of my discovery of fire. I was educating myself regarding the conflagration of matches, under my bed sheet, at my grandmother's house. While the experience had a magical quality at the moment, tell-tale burn marks in the tented sheets of my bed (as reported by my grandmother to her daughter, my mother) earned me the prompt promise of a true beating. As soon as we arrived back home at Cola City. Exiled to my room to await my punishment, I waited. Our mother was making dinner, and I continued to wait for the promised beating. Placed in proper perspective, our mother's beatings were legendary. She used the proper instrument, a pine bed slat some three and a half feet long by three inches wide, applied liberally to an exposed and quivering backside. Thus she dispensed justice in equal portions of humiliation and pain. Awaiting this outcome for many hours, I resolved I would wait no longer. The window was there, a cool evening invited, I was thru it and gone in a heartbeat. By prior agreement, I told Thomas I would wait for him if he chose to join me, in what would be our longest, farthest runaway episode, lasting four days, five nights. Better prepared, we could have gone further, longer. We still flee our past, those thoughts, words, deeds that pursue the child in each of us. Until we stop running, stand and turn to face that nameless terror that pursues us to the grave. We stop, turn to face Fear. And we say: No more. I am unafraid, forever.

An uneasy truce prevailed for a time in our childhood home. Ultimately they would resume their rule and dominion over us; we would resume our submission. The beatings would recede for a time at least, in a lingering overcast of fear. We were free for a brief moment, to consider a childhood of imaginings, of dreams, and of hope.

I try to remember now, why we ran away then. But it was, and is, very elemental. We ran to escape. We ran to escape our circumstances and our history, a history of proprietors who were never the lost parents of our hearts. We ran to escape our anguish of being unloved. And, we feared, unlovable. After all, our true parents had given us away to caretakers; and we seemed to fade away into a landscape of uncaring, indifference, anonymity. As our identities became mingled with the lost, we learned merely to survive in a bleak and hostile land, the features of which shifted and changed as we watched, even beneath our own feet. There was never firm ground beneath our children's feet. Our lives wore a perpetual shroud of doubt, uncertainty, and fear. And so we ran. It didn't matter where. This flight into, and down a muddy Oklahoma river, was a wistful hope to be the independent orphans like Huck Finn, himself an orphan. Living, thriving even, on a river. Freedom, and a light heart, lived on that river of our dreams, and it would embrace us, and all orphans, in loving arms and carry us to a better day, a brighter future. As we were learning survival skills, we were struggling to be the children we were, in a world that looked on us as orphans, and the cast-off children of parents unable to provide love, care, and simple human kindness. Our identities as orphans, as lost children, were who we were, and our true selves. We acquired masks to wear, disguising us as normal kids within a normal kid's life. We did not, could not, betray that we were lost children, beyond the reach or interest of the world. Ours was an insulated reality, a cocoon that shielded us from the pain, the anguish of uncaring.

And so, that muddy river has carried its orphan children into the here and now, of adulthood. The aging men of very young boys, men who can finally open their arms and hearts, to the lost children they were. Perhaps to open a door, perhaps a smile, laughter, something good to eat, and a place to rest, for the lost boys that have finally, and at long last, come home. As the man welcomes, embraces the child he was, larger arms than his own, enfold man and child. The lost child, and man, are found. The unloved and unlovable, loved. We float still, down that muddy endless river of dreams beneath a perfect blue sky.

ROLY POLY

From my earliest days, I cannot remember her face, my natural mother. I grasp for fragments of memory, like fragments from a dream you cannot recall, yet her face, her memory eludes me. As does the memory of our early home and family. I think she loved me, an important thing to a very young child. I seem to remember being held in her arms, carried and protected by her, but I cannot remember a single detail of her eyes, her face, or the larger being that was my mother. Only that narrow thread, a wistful hope perhaps that somehow love lived there in her mother's heart.

I do not remember being taken from her. Oddly, I do remember a large, flat, featureless building that warehoused myself, my brother, and a large number of lost children, also recent orphans, like us. Cots lined up dormitory-style, in each a young child. We were fed, and clothed, which was beyond our mother's ability, I am told.

An early memory from this place: I am walking down a long sidewalk in front of our new orphanage home. I am age two, and quite close to the ground, my legs are so short, but they seem to carry me well. The day is bright and warm, the sound of a lanyard bangs against a flagpole, echoes, resonating on the wind. My senses are tuned to this day, this place and time, and I feel very much alive.

I see a perfect tiny grey ball at my feet, on the sidewalk. A perfect small ball, such an uncommon shape in nature, but here at my feet, like a present. I am instantly fascinated. I carefully inspect it, and place it in my hand for a closer look. A complete mystery, its grey surface has perfect striations over its entire surface. I bring it within inches of my face, marveling at its lovely symmetry, and perfect proportion. Perfection is here in my tiny hand.

In an explosion of movement, my perfect miniature ball opens, and there is nothing but a writhing mass of tentacle legs, reaching for my face mere inches away. The shock I feel is exactly like electricity lighting up every cell in my small body. I would scream, but I cannot breathe. I scamper back as fast as a toddler's legs can carry me, to the relative safety of the dormitory, though I was at a loss to describe what had happened. The sheer physical shock of the moment remains transfixed in memory even now, seventy years later. Nothing before, or since, has quite that absolute clarity of moment.

My first meeting with a harmless, common roly poly (meal bug) remains the most vivid memory of my young life, possibly my entire life. Adrenalin-laced, it seems to spark memories of that strangest of places, and times, the orphanage. And yet, my mother's face remains undiscovered in the featureless landscape of early memory. And if you can forgive the repetition, I do seem to remember love that lived there, even if all else is lost, and adrift in time. And if there is value of any kind in our memory, perhaps, and possibly there is also value in what we cannot remember, in that mysterious, unapproachable dark night of the soul.

The point I must consider is not, that as a young child, I was terribly frightened by a common bug. That is simple irony and little else. The larger context of the bug episode, is that the world of a two year old child is suddenly, irrevocably shattered. This child I was finds himself without a home, parents, or family. He awakens from childhood dreams to find he is holding a nightmare, a thing that is unrecognizable in its sheer horror. Shock, like putting your finger into a live socket, is the experience of his moment, and his two year old mind is not yet equipped to handle circumstances beyond his understanding. The scars this young child acquired then, still live with him as a part of who he is and his experience in this world. An orphan suddenly living among other orphans, all children that lost their footing in their fragile world, and were swept away to a place where children are warehoused.

In some ways, I lament this child and all children who are displaced, and lost. In other ways, I recall that miracles still exist, as I am one myself, a miracle of survivability. At seventy years, I have lived long and well, a life of countless mistakes, not a few regrets. A miracle myself, I seem to encounter other miracles, like spring's first Tiger Swallowtail playing hide and seek behind me. He returns to his first drink, as a winged glory, from a large mud puddle. And too, from my porch, I am captured by a clear, high perfect note. Its author reveals himself, a common brown wren, as he launches his perfect, brief song upward into the cold air. The sun ascends through the pines, light enters a dark world, and warmth engages a cold one. Like the child I was, I find in this unaccountably strange place, unexpected moments of perfection. I do not know their source or purpose, only that they are resplendent and occur almost casually. I track the wisps, fragments of all those moments I miss, I celebrate those I do not miss.

Thus I track my own trajectory thru an awkward, ill-fitting life whose purpose even now eludes me. But I see if not clearly, an early swath of destruction, like the path of a tornado thru trees, to a place like this. A place of calm and relative quiet, where I can take notice of small glories that permeate this place and time. They are not far off, only just at hand. The curious flight of leaves thru air, floating, twirling, spinning, tumbling. Brilliance of green reflected in sunlight. Birdsong, impossibly pure and perfect, rises like the sun thru early dawn. And I, of course, a survivor at last, carrying in my soul the affliction of a thousand scars well earned in childhood. But a mystery beyond my grasp, as I leave to consider the numberless small glories of this day, itself a glory.

BOOGEY MAN

Before we were runaways, we were very young orphans. I cannot recall her face, a foster mother of our early years. But I recall a faded, cotton print dress, over features round and short. She was always holding a baby in one arm. She smelled good, and we were drawn to her maternal ways like two moths to a flame. She was our foster mother for a year, at ages three and five. The orphanage sought to place their orphans in a more natural family setting. Stays with foster parents were limited to twelve months, to preclude attachments between foster kids and foster parents, who were reimbursed for their efforts with a government stipend. Grocery money to feed the larger family.

But this young mother in her faded cotton dress, rocking her baby on the grey porch in front of us, was a real mother, a good mother. My three year old heart was smitten. She smiled and spoke to us with kindness and compassion. Her rooster was a very different matter.

Our new foster home was a faded, aging farmhouse somewhere in rural Oklahoma in 1951. A single light bulb graced the front porch, attracting all manner of moths and nocturnal bugs. Unbroken forest bordered the back of the house; our foster father routinely retreated into these woods, to return with wild honey. In the front a dirt road, and a large chicken pen containing a variety of fowls, including a large rooster. We were at eye level, the rooster and I, as I sought the outhouse conveniently located inside the chicken pen. The farmhouse did not have its own bathroom, in rural Oklahoma of 1951. Rooster's plumage was regal and brilliant, large yellow eyes exuded challenge and ferocity to all comers. I was no match, as I fled to the safety of the outhouse, Rooster in full pursuit. My cries for rescue brought Thomas, again and again, to escort me to safety beyond the reach of the avenging fowl. There was no middle ground, no compromise. If I required the bathroom, I must run the gauntlet of Rooster's wrath, Tyrant of the chicken pen and outhouse. My whimpers and timidity inflamed his ferocity, as he launched himself toward me with two inch leg spurs, and three inch beak to my exposed legs. I may have screamed, such was my terror, I can't quite remember. But a young life replete with humiliation had found a new level. Rooster became the gold standard of my living terror. I narrowly survived the gauntlet of the outhouse, as Thomas tired of providing safety escort, beyond the reach of Rooster's violence.

Our foster mom, I wish I remembered her name, provided maternal safety. I hovered close, hoping she would not vanish as our last mother had. I could endure the rooster, and much more, if I could keep her as my mother. She bragged to neighbors that I was "her little biscuit-eater", a reference to my capacity for wild honey and biscuits. I positively glowed in the kindness of her praise. Life was good here with her, at long last, but it was not to last. We were to be farmed out to other foster families in other places. The ground beneath our feet ever shifting, never secure as we were handed out to strangers, by other strangers in our charge, none of whom I knew. The loose, shifting sand we stood on seemed to be sliding down an endless mountain, carrying two young orphans, three and five years old, to an uncertain and precarious future. I hoped there would be a future for Thomas and I. We hoped against hope.

Meanwhile, it was bedtime on the farm. Thomas and I were given a small bare room in the back of the house, bordering the tall, dark forest. House rules were simple. Bed time meant you went to bed, stayed there, and fell asleep "before the boogeyman got you". This was immeasurably troubling to a three year old mind. Adult rules, were precepts beyond question. I peered fearfully out the small bedroom window into dark woods, searching for a lurking, fearsome presence that hunted, and carried away, unsleeping children. My child's mind clothed him in rags, a long dark coat with teeth like fangs, wide-brimmed hat covering a face that was not human. He is the Boogeyman. He lives in the deep woods of children's minds, his lust for children's flesh rapacious and legendary, and he was looking for me as surely as I was looking for him. I fell asleep as quietly, suddenly as a light switch is turned off. Thus I survived each night till the next, the certain terror always looming in the darkness outside the window.

Our young foster mother could not have known that her bedtime promptings inspired such terror in her temporary child. My adult mind has measured the time, the people, the circumstances, and clothed them in the faded cotton print of memory and forgiveness. Our vanished foster mother, her rooster, her boogeyman, my fear, terror, and longing for a real family. All clothed now in time, memory, forgiveness. Even Thomas, who saved a child-brother from a wicked rooster, and a more wicked boogeyman, and the thousand terrors that inhabited and thrived in our Netherlands of childhood. All cloaked now in the very special fabric of time, memory, and forgiveness.

And so, time distills human fear, suffering, and misery into something else, something that is not suffering, terror, and not fear, something that is more benign. We look back at the horror of our history and smile. Time is transfigurative as we rise from the ashes of our own destruction, like the mythical Phoenix. We spread our new, vast wings born of fire and destruction, rise to embrace the rising sun before us, and the larger, immeasurable firmament blazing with the light of a thousand suns, we rise. We pause in flight, a rising splendor and glory, to view our fragile beginnings . . . Joy erupts from our wings like flashes of lightning, as we rise with speed, power and passion into the awaiting embrace of infinitude. We rise.

WILLOW TREE

I remember that all houses had alleys behind them when I was growing up. Unpaved and unpretentious, they were simple one-lane dirt paths that housed garbage cans for weekly pickup. People walked their dogs, kids made rapid destinations between two houses, or twenty. My brother Thomas and I visited these darkened allies at night, as our parents and the rest of the world slept unaware. In a daytime world of perennial subjugation, these alleys became our nocturnal freedom. A cool night air might beckon us, and we were dressed and gone on cat feet, from our second story bedroom window. We were fugitive acrobats, pursuing the perfect crime of freedom, as we negotiated a silent passage along high rooflines, ledges and walls to the ground. If our parents ever knew, their knowledge remained their secret, as our secret remained ours.

There are deeper much darker secrets that remain guarded to this day in this house. Norman and Sadie, odd Midwestern names, were our adoptive parents. Cecil AKA Sweetie, the family bulldog, was a female dog. She was white with touches of black on her low powerful frame. I thought then, and now, that Sweetie was the better guardian, friend and protector. The better parent of awkward, adopted young children that we were. Sweetie so named for her sweet disposition to all people, but especially to Thomas and myself, her very special children whom she watched with unfailing devotion and love. Her massive chest housed an even larger heart of love. Thomas and I were

19

both shocked and thrilled, when Sweetie bit our mother as she was attacking us with a switch, for an unremembered crime.

Darker secrets visited our childhood home. Adopted at the age of four and six, Thomas and I had guarded prospects of a happy childhood. Our parents early efforts at parenting were sincere at first, though lacking that simple ingredient of love, which our dog had in great measure. Norman brought home, from a short business trip, a toy stamped metal train, complete with an oval metal track. A train to nowhere, I was mesmerized by its sheer size, power and the "Santa Fe" emblazoned on its graceful yellow flanks. This was a real train that went perpetually on a track that had no end. And I, the favored child, was brought a true and special treasure, my brother slighted with a lesser, unremembered gift. What there was of it, I basked in the glow of a favorite son, even if deeper bonds of trust and love failed.

A giant willow tree graced a fenced back yard of our first true home on Little Lane. I remember only now, that it was our first true home at four and six years old. The house was small, humble in demeanor, but clean, and large enough to grow a child's hopes and dreams, from a past that did have hope but rarely dreams, such was the raw bleakness of our early years. If our young spirits were beaten down by the apparent whim of circumstances, they were not totally crushed and destroyed. Thus is the true sheer resilience in the souls of the young. Life then seemed a balancing act, as we teetered ever more precariously, with what we felt was oblivion itself. There was never sure and certain footing in our early years, never a place that would house our hearts, bring our young minds a simple measure of peace and quiet contentment.

My refuge was the tall graceful willow tree of our backyard. The yard was otherwise sterile of all shrubs, flowers and plants, only grass. The willow was enough, I retreated to its flowing limbs with its elongated green leaves that caressed like fingers, as they held me in their branches that felt like tender arms, held me and loved me, there in that quiet place. I would become lost to a world that I was already lost to, but in the enfolding and embracing arms of the weeping willow tree, I was cocooned and safe from a harsh and uncaring world. Soft green leaves touched my skin with the delicacy of compassion, healing all pain. If love was missing in the larger world of a childhood, it was found, at last, in the enfolding arms of the willow tree. A place where I was safe, hidden from view, where I was caressed and loved, in the arms of the willow tree. For a time I would live in those green and flowing branches, from which nothing was missing.

My world, my being complete, my soul in repose as I watched sunlight streaming through high branches of my willow tree, while I lay both hidden and held. In a world that was not safe, I was safe here in the elegant beauty of my willow tree.

At last, I dreamed dreams of a shining land that lived just on the horizon. I could almost see it, it was a short distance, just on the horizon of a young boys dream.

A place of light, of joy, of happiness, the willow tree protected me now. I viewed that land of dreams, through a child's eyes in my willow, just on the horizon, not too far, emanating light and joy and laughter, what was its name..... I can name it, this place of dreams and light. **Donald Duck Land**, that's the place I can almost see, I can visit there just on the horizon. It is a place of light filled with characters of light. Donald Duck and his wife, Daisy Duck, she wears a large ribbon atop her head, and has brown eyes with impossibly long eyelashes. Daisy has a feminine charm and simplicity of spirit which has the quality of joy itself. There also lives Goofy and Pluto, the dog, and a population of happy souls filled with laughter and surrounded by light in a land of dreams. I seemed to touch the boundaries of this place without ever entering, but I realized that anything could be found there.

Everything that was missing here, lived there in that place where there was no twilight and no darkness. Every delightful hope here, lived there, in that place of dreams. I viewed it from my willow tree, as sunlight streamed through high branches, in an endless Oklahoma summer at a small house on Little Lane. Time has passed, much time, this young child has become old, the willow branches he looked through have become the eyes of an old man, who merely remembers.

Remembers the child lost but embraced by the willow tree, remembers the land of dreams and light almost visited then by a young child. I look out from an old man's eyes now, through spring branches of my birch tree. I think of the child, his land of dreams, and I remember.

FIRST GRADE: A DAY IN THE LIFE

Before my career as a runaway, I visited and grew to love the creek that flowed at the bottom of the hill. It had a gracefully arced, wooden bridge that I would pause on, to view the clear water below. The water was alive with life itself; it mesmerized me with its fluid textures. Long, emerald green mosses, and algae lived there, long green tresses articulated the graceful flow of these living waters. I viewed here, perfection, as I studied the depths, for tiny minnows, or a prized crayfish. Unseen treasures lived here, blue damsel flies flirted in the reeds, larger dragon flies patrolled the skies above the creek, like miniature jet fighters. The creek was my reward for sitting six hours in first grade classroom. I remember a distant chaos of sound and movement of chairs and children, all eventually aligned to face the rising sun, of an unremembered teacher. I searched the warehoused children there for a face that might seem familiar. It was springtime, the sun was shining on the tall mature pines that ringed and encircled the playground. Recess bell rang, one hundred very small children charged the narrow doorway that led to absolute and perfect freedom of the school yard. I am the Lone Ranger, I hear myself announcing above the tumult. "Who wants to be Tonto?" Thirty hands shoot up in the air: "Me, me, me, me, me," a perfect syncopated chorus of volunteers for the job of Tonto, all hopping with an enthusiasm that overwhelms me. I pick out the nearest, trusting face. "You're Tonto." To the beleaguered rest I anoint: "All of you are Deputy Sheriffs. A very big role. We have to go get the bad guys." "Where are they," a dozen voices respond, swiveling heads in search of the bad men. This posse is ready to ride, I think. "They are holed up in those tall pines, at the other end of the playground." Thirty kids, all on horseback, thunder down the playground to serve up some true justice to the bad guys. I am riding a wave of pure energy, my thundering posse around me, and my faithful Indian companion, Tonto, beside me. The sun is shining on a brilliant spring day, justice, truth, the good, may yet prevail, as a human wave breaks on the shores of the tall pines that hide the bad guys. I try to direct this pure focused energy to its proper purpose. "Find the bad guys, they're in these trees, find them!" The pure wave breaks, and scatters now on the shores, my thirty sheriffs run off, with Tonto, each one in a different direction. I think . . ., they just don't fully grasp a good plot. And I, the Lone Ranger, return alone to unremembered walls of classrooms that would house and contain our early years. My career as the Lone Ranger flounders and is forgotten in the clear and perfect passion of the moment, in a child's life.

My Lone Ranger career stalled, I view Cindy, a round and perfect 6 year old, who likes pink chiffon dresses. Cindy is no tomboy, but the quintessential girly girl. I think I like her, I'm just not too sure about the dress. It's pink. It seems to accentuate her roundness, like a dressed up Easter egg. Part of me recoils, that's too much pink on too much roundness. She looks at me as I ponder these paradoxes. And she smiles a smile of pure sweetness. I like Cindy; I like the pink chiffon encasing roundness. I am invited to her sixth birthday party, our date is set. I have never been to a girl's birthday party. I have never been to any birthday party, the etiquette of such grand events a mystery. This may be how people get married and start a family. It is unfamiliar terrain; I hesitate, approaching her small house above a steeply embanked yard. I am buoyed up, remembering her smile emblazoned in pink. I knock, her house is full of kids, none of whom I know. I find Cindy in the middle of her birthday melee; she is swathed in pink that seems to fluoresce with an inner brightness. I search for her perfect smile that has brought me here to her door, a hesitant suitor, for the heart of Cindy. She glances my way, her eyes brush over me with swift irreverence. Hope sinks, and within it, my heart. I wait, I know she will not come to greet me, or even look at me again, with her pink smile. This is a strange place filled with strangers. I will not look at Cindy, because she will not look at me. And so, in angry resolution, I leave; realize I do not like roundness in pink chiffon. A wounded young heart retreats to find the balm of beauty, the splendid isolation of clear, flowing water. These are my companions and my true love, the ripple and caress of the stream, silver minnows swimming through emerald moss. Small green leopard frogs vanishing from sight in the fluid forest. I dream a dream, it is this place, this time, this moment, sun shining on clear water, a thousand hidden creatures, like secrets in these green, moving forests that flow like water. I find life, even perfection, here in this moment, in simple beauty, as spring sun shines down on secret forests that move in water.

THE GIFT

She was young, sweet, kind and my favorite second grade teacher. She spoke to me and actually listened, a revelation to me. She watched me with her large clear eyes and smiled a smile that lingers still in my memory.

So captured by kindness and a simple human quality, I resolved that I should bring her a gift. It should be special to celebrate our special friendship. She would look at it and her heart would smile. A special gift to her, a true reflection of a special fondness and true, pure affection.

I began to look for my special gift, I noticed the vast mulberry tree with its interesting leaves and numberless lobed berries ranging from red to nearly black. Black mulberries were ripe and succulent, though they required a careful inspection to remove the tiny white mites that enjoyed their lobed landscape. I would pause to capture ripe berries on my way to elementary school, a tart sweetness that was interesting and delightful.

I thought, I will bring her fresh mulberries from this large tree, picked by me for her. She will see their dark, lobed beauty and smile. My heart suddenly exuberant at this perfect, small gift.

A riddle presents, what to carry my ripe berries in to protect their delicate ripeness. Presentation is everything. My resources limited to a backpack, I use clean white school paper folded into an envelope, choice berries inside like dark jewels. They rode in a special place in my backpack to her desk. It was early, my special moment now, a gift to a favorite teacher. A giddy excitement as I tell her I have something special for her. She smiles her wonderful smile, large eyes inviting me into a rare moment.

I retrieve my prize; I notice a dark red stain on carefully folded corners. She hesitates, her wonderful smile frozen. I help her unwrap her present, I am not sure now what resides inside, a despairing hope that my ripe berries are still lovely. "I picked them myself on my way to school." I unfold the paper, explaining what I hope she will find. She recoils, is it fear or terror or simple panic, her smile now a lost wonder. I view now an unrecognizable catastrophe, my simple gift. The arduous journey proved too difficult, my ripe mulberries a dark red, bleeding mess. I can offer no explanation to assuage her fear now. This may have been a small animal, a pet perhaps, now exploded in my white paper, red secretions covered the inside. I needed to leave now, no words to explain the visible horror inside.

Her clear shock had frozen on her face as I vanish ghostlike. Remembering her and our moment, I suggest a clear knowledge of a special gift that she will remember always. My favorite teacher, her heart given the instruction of fear, an unexpected reward for an unexpected gift.

BROWN SHOES

Time to patch up these old shoes again; a third grader can put on a lot of miles and much wear. This has become routine, placing pieces of cardboard inside both shoes to cover the gaping holes in the soles. The holes patched with cardboard are slightly less visible. Humbling to be wearing shoes with holes for months to school and church. Our mother encourages patches, new shoes are not a consideration. My adoptive parents drive two cars; we live in a nice house in a well groomed neighborhood, and I wear shoes with holes to school that I patch with cardboard. That is the landscape of this world, and so I wear my patches and my humility with practiced obscurity that will not bring notice to myself and my holes. I ask for new shoes for my Birthday, a month away, and a shining new pair appear at the appointed time, Birthday shoes. They are wonderful, brown shining leather, everything about them seems to radiate a resplendent newness. It is almost overwhelming, my new brown shoes. Nothing can compare, my shame, the humble badge of wearing shoes with holes, it fades in the shiny glow of new leather.

My third grade teacher must see my new shoes; she will see their splendor, as I do, and be impressed, as I am. I have a boyhood crush on her, she towers over me with a smile of pure kindness. She is young, pretty and has a red nose from chronic sneezing. She regards me with a rare interest and compassion that is like the balm of Gilead in a dry desert land. I drink deeply of these waters, taste the manna of this moment. The moment itself separates from time and becomes resplendent and shining. She asks about my new shoes, I venture forward into the moment, then retreat. The light is too bright; I got them for my Birthday. My soul laid bare before her, I trust her kindness, it is the quality of mercy. She seems to see all of me, not just the shining new shoes. She sees my confession, the holes, the hope, the poverty of my young spirit. She crouches before me, her eyes look into mine. I avert my gaze; the tenderness of the moment is beyond my grasp. I am defeated, wounded by kindness, my soul laid bare, scars of a thousand days cleansed, anointed. She looks in my eyes, a smile, that fragile perfect kindness descends. It is over as quickly as it happened. She turns in a pirouette, a dancer, our moment lost but imprisoned in time. She has seen my secret, the lost child, with a smile of radiant kindness, and then retreated. She will fade now into a familiar landscape of my childhood even as I remember a quality of mercy framing the moment, all remembered in the living heart of a child.

Edwin, my friend, is playing jacks with the girls in the playground at school on a shaded porch. It is a puzzle that Edwin is my friend, all the other boys are running and shouting on the playground in the perfect noisy melee of boyhood.

My friend Edwin plays jacks with the girls here in the cool of a shaded school porch, oblivious to the frenzy all about him. He's a picture of composure with his red hair and red freckles, an odd but interesting portrait here in a shaded corner of the school yard. I am aware of the perceptive cruelty of the swarm of young boys, my approach and contact with Edwin with red hair, is guarded and secretive. He smiles an open and confident smile and I am drawn into the narrow arms of friendship with Edwin. He is unlike any boy in my memory. He has pale limbs and he does not compete in the contests of budding virility with other boys.

He wants to be a Librarian when he grows up, another oddity I think, and he plays jacks with girls with fluid dexterity. Edwin my friend, a puzzle, a paradox and mystery, invites me to have lunch at his home. A first for me, Edwin lives very close to an old elementary school, our school. He walks home for lunch each day to a lunch prepared by a mother who loves doing so for her son. The rest of the school eats from brown paper bags brought from home, like so many cats. Edwin, my new friend is given special treatment, like a young red haired royalty or prince.

I think this will be a special occasion, so I must present myself well. My hair is dry, wild and unkempt. I must look well groomed for lunch with Edwin, prepared by his mother for a son well loved. I secrete a small bottle of liquid hair emollient, Butch Wax, to give me a properly groomed appearance for lunch with Edwin. Under the guise of washing my hands for lunch, I retreat to the bathroom for a liberal dousing of liquid Butch Wax for my unruly hair. The change is dramatic and frightening, I have put far too much liquid wax on my hair. I now have a corpse like appearance, my hair is flattened and dripping with an oily shine. I panic at my new and shocking appearance, at the gravity of my error. I try washing off the waxy excess that drips onto my face and my shoulders. It will not wash off, it is wax and needs sterner measures than plain water. Edwin waits and wonders why washing my hands should take ten minutes. Toilet paper is totally useless, so I use all the hand towels within reach to soak up the disaster on my head. The towels, all of them, seem to work as I leave at last to join Edwin at a stalled lunch. He looks at me, shocked at the sudden change, my head a gleaming, waxed dome, every hair glued against my scalp in waxy submission. I avert my eyes in pure embarrassment, Edwin defers comment. We eat sandwiches on white bread in silence and return to school. I am not invited back to Edwin's house for lunch. I consider the waxy destruction of bathroom towels left in the wake of my misadventure and know this is the reason.

Our new friendship has a new blight, and I wonder if anyone in school will notice my new and interesting appearance. I blend into the halls and classrooms of third grade with a practiced anonymity. This is a new and interesting time, I pause in flight to consider new possibilities. A new me, a better me perhaps, in Butch Wax and new brown shoes. As a new summer emerges from a cold winter's sleep at the old elementary school, in the life of a young boy.

SPEED

I am traveling down a long downhill grade at high speed that is increasing. I am riding an olive green, three speed Raleigh Racer, an English built bicycle. It looks fast and it is fast, with a blistering top speed beyond the reach of all the neighborhood standard bikes, with their fat balloon tires and comfy seats. I am riding to my old elementary school, my daily ride and marveling at the sheer speed and velocity of this special bicycle, built in England. Metal stampings and decals announce to all its special origins, purpose and mission. Its olive green trim flanks suggests military grade, a precision and purpose built speed machine. It speeds me down the street on its skinny racing tires with fearsome velocity as I crouch low on its thin racing seat to minimize wind resistance. I'm as fast as most cars, I think, on these sleepy neighborhood streets. Faster than anything on two wheels, nothing can catch me, I bet. The wind tears at my eyes and face as I approach the old elementary school at fabulous speed. Skinny tires hum a song of pure speed, time does slow with great speed, Einstein I think.

There is a rusting, heavy chain that blocks all traffic on the side street beside the old elementary school. Kids can walk around the chain or duck underneath, bicyclist must do the same. I usually stop, get off and duck underneath the chain. Today, my adrenalin and speed enhanced brain consider, what if I duck under the chain while still riding? Stay right to the high side of the chain, crouch low and

I'm through. This is dangerous, possibly even a heroic act, I feather the brakes for the upcoming turn, there is loose gravel, the chain is immediately there, face high. I see the heavy rusting links holding a sagging sign in the middle of the road. I must duck now; the chain seems to reach for me. My speed is too great and it's too late to brake. I move now like an out of control rocket. My body freezes in space, all control lost, I hit the heavy chain like a speeding bullet, my neck snaps the chain as if it were a thread. I barely felt it, my speed is undiminished. I wonder if they will ask who broke the school chain. I slow to a coast on the uphill ride, get off my bike as I arrive at the school. I look back at the chain, it is broken clearly and lying on the ground across the road, the sign also lying on the ground in defeat like a dead animal. My neck is unmarked and undamaged. I am suddenly, grandly heroic, I've done something never done before in all the old elementary school's August history. Possibly in any school in this city. I smile, enjoying the pure spectacle of an unlikely, perhaps impossible event. This is the first and only time I have confessed to this act, the breaking of the school chain and school rules prohibiting the breaking of said chain. I tell no one, not even my best friend, that it was me, that I broke the chain. My heart basks in the glow of a solitary heroism.

Recounting this story so many years later, I advise the young boy I was with a cautionary: I hope we do not get into trouble.

LOITA

Loita is the girl next door. It's in the full bloom of a hot Oklahoma summer, as we talk over the low hedge that separates our houses. As an only child, she is my age, but I never see her in the old elementary school. I think she goes to another school, possibly one for the gifted. Loita is a tall, thin girl with short red hair that frames a pleasant face full of freckles. Freckles seem to overflow down both arms, I think of a spotted trout in clear water. She has a prepubescent glow about her that at once captures my interest and imagination. I wonder if there may be a future with Loita and her red hair and freckles, like a spotted trout. She holds arms folded neatly before her, her hands move in graceful arcs, fingers articulate her conversation, like a teacher before a classroom. These private conversations over the low hedge seem to be of great import to me, a valuable part of this day. She talks well and at length, with a true authority of someone who simply knows. She discretely acknowledges that hers is a high IQ and I believe her tacitly. She was Loita after all, with a uniqueness of carriage, grace, and style that transcended her name and our summer talks over the low hedge between our houses. There was mystery here, if I could crack it, but like capturing butterflies, my summer avocation, it required equal measures of determination and subtlety. Loita was a rare butterfly with red wings, she could fly at any moment to evade capture, so I waited with a rare patience. Listening carefully to her unique tones and inflections of word, as her fingers moved in graceful arcs, like a conductor at a symphony. She moved with an uncommon erectness, rigidity even, her steps even and measured, Heir to the throne of royalty I considered, clearly superior to commoners such as myself. A clear travesty, I watched in muted silence as her mother swatted her back through the hedge when she ventured to far into the foreign terrain of my back yard. She hopped at the measured impact, scampering back to her house and vanishing there for a time.

I waited for Loita, in subtle ways, to resume our summer conversation over the low hedge. Passage into each other's yard required parental permission, eyes tracked our interactions, so to early detect unseemly interest between royalty and a commoner like myself. I do not recall ever touching Loita's white freckled skin, her presence sufficient to my interest. Our conversation compelling and vibrant, we did not require the usual games of pursuit and capture of lesser kids who might feign disinterest in our lofty conversations. Words, animation, and laughter flowed like water over crystalline depths. Loita would introduce me to the world of ideas, the articulation of the unspoken. An important clue to the mystery of Loita, her grasp and easy grace of intangibles, far more compelling than simple form. Invisible ideas plucked from midair, and celebrated, perhaps a first in my young life. There was brilliance to Loita, she was herself brilliant and graceful as arcs of her fingers in midair seemed to point the way.

I lingered surreptitiously along the low hedges between our houses, as though in silent signal between us. She rarely, if ever appeared as I waited, she was doing more important things. Surrendering my vigil by the hedge, Loita would appear always, at moments unexpected, her face with a glow like our conversations. Perhaps there could be a future with Loita, a very different future from any imagining.

COOKOUT

I am going, Thomas and I, to Loita's cookout in her backyard, a first for us both.

An unexpected honor of the highest order, we are the only guests there. I think it is Loita's Birthday, her tenth, and she exudes an elegance and poise far beyond her years. She is mature and wise; her face radiates a happy contentment. Cats - eyeglasses, the current rage, and generous freckles meet in a pleasant paradox, all framed in short, very red hair. Freckles that swim on her arms like a spotted trout. A masterpiece if not classical beauty, no less a masterpiece in ....Loita. At once both ordinary and extraordinary.

I consult with my warden who poses as my adoptive mother. She signs off on this outing next door with a stern and final warning: "You are to eat one hamburger and only one, not two, not three, one! If they offer you more than one you will thank them and refuse. Do not forget, I will tell you this only once. Do you understand, one burger!" A sudden chill descends, a celebration turns somber. This is a very serious woman, I decide, as I notice the large black binoculars sitting at hand on the window sill. Her second floor sitting room provides an expansive view of Loita's back yard and our own. She scarcely needs the binoculars, but she will be able to see clearly and consider our choice of condiments, as well as a useful count of chips we consume.

We have no birthday gift for Loita, on a short invitation, her parents graciously defer. Our eyes hungrily search the grill as the smoky aroma makes our mouths water uncontrollably. We are inmates, confined to the prison of one burger today. No exceptions. I dare not look at the window my mother now watches me from, but I feel her eyes following every movement and any intent. I try to appear calm and composed, but I am merely frozen under her fierce scrutiny. This celebration suddenly feels like punishment, I cannot share Loita's joy in this, her moment. I am suddenly ravenous, my only thought, the grill overflowing with small burgers and hot dogs, the dense aroma of searing meats wafting about my head and nose and rising skyward into the summer heat. My stomach rumbles to the rasp and buzz of cicadas in midsummer. My hosts, Loita's parents, have a kind and solicitous manner that is captivating. I devour my small burger with the rapacity of a starving dog, chips help with the deficit. We are finished, Thomas and I, just as our kind hosts are beginning. The binoculars rake us like machine gun fire, we are pinned in her sites, like insects under a microscope.

"Have another burger, they're small; we have plenty. A hot dog?" our hosts plead, seeing our clear hunger, to eat. A thought appears, we are taught manners, would it not seem ill mannered to refuse our gracious host's offer of more? They show us a well-stocked grill, brevity commands the moment. We hesitate, the binoculars view their offer and our dilemma. I send a kind of a signal with my eyes to them, trying to convey our predicament of being watched, our one-burger sentencing, a clear and final edict. Their kindness and our hunger have conspired to our doom. We eat a second small burger gratefully, under clear penalty of certain death as the binoculars watch. We will desperately affirm: "Her parents made us eat our second burger, there was a two-burger minimum at Loita's cookout". Loita's father is eating his second and planning on a third at least.

Loita's parents remarkable kindness have condemned us to an early, untimely demise, in this, our final meal. But full of the twin mercies of kindness and of food, we are better prepared to meet our maker. I consider it well worth it. It was an excellent burger, especially the second one. So, we finally and at last celebrate Loita's birthday, a rare young woman and my friend. There are numerous things here to celebrate; the fateful second burger, the blossoming of Loita, and our wonderful hosts that fed us from their table of immeasurable bounty.

We celebrate our survival to this moment, to enjoy this excellent burger among friends, in full view of a tyrant who sees all of this and will crush us (in due time) the moment our celebration draws to a close and we must return. We celebrate our moment, the moment celebrates us, we rise above this time, above our struggle and humble beginnings. We rise to celebrate the fall of all tyrants who crush the innocent. On eagle's wings we rise to view our beginning, our present, our end, our hearts rise like smoke above the world, beyond ourselves. We celebrate all things, impossible things, we celebrate us. We celebrate the true and perfect excellence of the second burger.

A DREAM OF FLIGHT

I liked trees; I liked climbing trees. They were a refuge and even play partners, accommodating our childhood interest and agility with a calm presence.

Summer cicadas with electric crescendos sang in high branches, drowning out all other sounds. Blue jays visit with militant calls, but this tree was ours. Young boys build fort tree houses, ours was a simple scrap of plywood supported by a level fork high in the branches. To get to our fort we climbed a vertical trunk with rungs nailed to the trunk.

We would need a swing, not a girl's swing with a seat, but a real swing.

Thirty feet of rope tied to the highest clear branch. It must be heavy, strong and climbable. Our father pressed into duty, the rope was of industrial grade hemp with a one inch diameter. Thomas, unafraid of height, climbed a precipitously tall branch to secure the high end. We could look into the second-story windows from that altitude. A knot tied to the lower end just off the ground to support feet, our rope was now functional art. It was breathtaking simply to look at, it would be thrilling to use. We climbed it like monkeys, viewed our high roofline and second-story windows. This was true adventure, but there was more. Our young minds had measured the distance between the fort and rope length. It was perfect. Sitting fifteen feet up in the tree fort, we could hold the rope end and swing in a perfect high arc of perhaps sixty feet, a pure thrill. We could peer into our parents second floor window, at the height of the swing from mere feet away.

We were gymnasts of the highest order, astronauts flirting with the edge of space. Our father, a co-conspirator in acquiring the rope, secured our mother's silence. We swung to freedom; the pure thrill ignited our hearts beyond all possibility. We swung from sky to earth and back again, we swung like a human pendulum to absurd heights, a furtive glance into a high bedroom window. Our hearts made glad in the pure delightful mixture of speed, height, danger and adrenaline. Forty years later I would launch my young daughter (sternly admonished to hang on for dear life) from a high hilltop, to rooftop and back, thus we were both addicted.

I dream a dream of flight, inspired by the moments of flight on the high swing. I had a simple conviction that I could fly like Peter Pan. I didn't require the risk of broken bones from great heights, mine would be ground skimming, mere inches from the ground, no less pure flight. A high hedge at the end of the yard, I reasoned a short, fast run followed by a horizontal dive, my groundspeed would allow me to clear the tall hedge. It should work if I could secure all elements, especially the more inscrutable ones involving mind over matter, into a working plan. Flying was in fact, simple. Bees did it, flies and birds did it. Peter Pan did it.

I can do it. A certain knowledge of flight as I had, implied or rather confirmed the fact, I can fly. The only thing remaining: to fly. I choreographed each step into a fluid movement, considering every detail to secure my perfect launch. A thought:

"Thomas if I jumped from this tree, ten feet up, could I fly?" "Yes," Thomas's measured response. My certain knowledge of pure flight tainted with an ugly suspicion, I query his judgment. "Go ahead," Thomas replies with a trace of anticipation. I paused in my distrust of humans, their plundering of innocence.

Nor did I launch myself onto the ground from running, as choreographed numberless times, the thought of grass burns too intrusive of my dream. Pure, perfect flight would wait for sleep and dreams, where my choreography worked, flying countless times, even a frightening flight far beyond the earth. No place to be lost, deep space, I returned home to earth.

Real flight would wait twenty years, as hang gliders were being conceived.

Young men like me, full of certain knowledge of flight, would run and fling themselves into space from high mountains, thus proving what every child knows.

Dreams can be real.

BLACK WIDOW

The next week my mother would inquire what I kept in a glass jar beside the house. My childhood passion and obsession was the capture of winged jewels in flight, that were to become part of a treasured collection of butterflies. Lesser, but interesting creatures would be offered a jar, or an aquarium. I had discovered my first black widow, that now enjoyed a sheltered life inside my jar. Black, beautiful, and deadly, her red hour glass spot confirmed her status as an ultimate predator. An ultimate prize, I marveled at the sheer, shiny blackness, and her tentative movements about her irregular web. I was unable to conceal the obvious, my mother awaited an answer. To her credit, she did display some consternation when told of my deadly prize, prompting its quick removal from the vicinity of the house. For just an instant, the balance of power shifted, I had the black widow on my side, my mother's fear empowering me. My widow released, I pursued less lethal creatures. Creatures that I secretly hoped would cause her, the tyrant mother, a moment of consternation, that boundless cruelty is not forever unnoticed, unrewarded, at its own hand.

SALAD DRESSING

Grandmother Carrie had always seemed old and infirm. She moved in a slow shuffling gate, expressionless with eyes downturned, seemingly to plot her path. There were rumors, in the old photos in the attic of a life full of interesting events and characters, in a time none of us would visit. These she kept to herself, well-guarded, so that we would never understand who she was and the experiences that created the aged woman before us. She had come to live with us in our home, due to her advancing years and infirmities, unable to take care of a century old home built by her family. The elegant home would become a rental until years later when my adoptive parents would move in for an early retirement.

For now, we all lived an interesting, if precarious balance at our second house in Cola City. Grandmother Carrie brought along Betsy, a black cocker spaniel. She seemed a reflection of our grandmother, nervous, retiring, not a dog that liked kids or anything about her new home. Betsy erred once in approaching our bulldog's food dish and a brief dog fight of splendid magnitude erupted, shocking all of us. Betsy retreating unhurt but defeated. Grandmother Carrie herself defeated by time, fading into obscurity and obsolescence, did not talk much nor did her dog ever run or play. She continually held her lower belly as though in late stage pregnancy. Her chief and desperate complaint to her daughter was her bowels. I think Grandmother Carrie had a clear premonition about her prospects of happiness and even survivability, in our house. Her prospects embraced us both. Her growing belly that she carried about housed a tumor the size of a softball that would shortly kill her. Betsy, her spaniel, would pass before her, anonymously and unloved.

Grandma holds a gallon glass milk jug, heavy in her frail fingers. Her strength fails, a full gallon of whole milk explodes, then blossoms over the kitchen vinyl floor like a white flower. A huge disaster, Thomas and I are eating breakfast, first row seats to view the spectacle. A moment of shock as our mother rushes in.

They move in concert to stem the white flood that threatens. "Milk is very good for vinyl floors," Grandma sagely asserts, a casual commentary to a catastrophe.

Thomas and I think, "Oh, that's good." I think I still believe that advice even now.

Weeks go by; Thomas and I are sitting at our tiny folding vinyl table. I sit in my high chair, it has folding metal steps that I never use, but still admire, this is my chair. Grandma is putting mayonnaise on our pretentiously tiny salads, frail hands rattle a spoon inside the mayo jar as Thomas and I look on. In retrospect, it was perhaps the rattle of the spoon retrieving a dollop of mayo, perhaps the view of the small salad awaiting its dressing, but Pavlovian, at the perfect and unlikely moment, a thin stream of saliva escapes Grandma's loose jowls and lands perfectly in my salad and disappears. Speechless silence, Grandma gives my salad several dismissive nudges with the mayo spoon. No one breathes, our mother is in the kitchen and has missed everything. Grandma will not venture forth to my rescue. I am alone and on my own. Children are seen, never heard in these primitive times. I must eat my salad as though nothing has happened. My brother watches fascinated, a mere trace of a smile. My interest in this food, any food, vanished. My mother oblivious, she is the enforcer of law, the law that now commands me to eat my salad. And so, in deepest repugnance, I eat my salad and its interesting dressing, as my brother watches in stunned delight.

Revenge, a dish best served cold, as I gained my revenge on both Thomas and Grandma. Thomas, by simply outrunning him on the long downhill stretch towards the old elementary school. I do not remember the provocation, there were many in our young lives.

He was in mortal pursuit, running with true vengeance and evil intent. I knew I must outgun the larger boy or face certain destruction. The faster boy, I out sped him and left him gasping in my wake. Once going the Raleigh bicycle could generate impressive speed, my trailing laughter a mockery in his ears that he would remember.

Once a month, our parents would vanish for the weekend, a peremptory goodbye and they were gone for the night. We celebrated, all of us. Grandma would make her personal favorite always, of rice and raisins, followed by ice cream floats. Then TV, again her choice of *The Champagne Music of Lawrence Welk,* a musical variety show that I found appalling, followed by *Gunsmoke,* a swaggering James Arness in Western leather. Lawrence Welk's heavy handed tactics in getting all the band members to smile all the time, struck me as degrading to the performers and insulting to viewers who must know the smiles were purely cosmetic and clearly enforced. Much as prisoners being required to smile despite their hard labor. "Sauerkraut Dick", so named for his serious manner and presence, owned and played a true treasure, *a* Stradivarius violin.

He played with a resonating purity and passion that eclipsed all performers before and after. He had no equal, his notes clear, vibrant, and perfect, seemed to hang in the air, even now, as a fitting tribute to perfection. I saw then that man could attain perfection by "Sauerkraut Dick", his surname an insult to his sublime virtuosity. His difficulty in smiling, though publicly prodded to do so, was a gesture of his humility in presenting to the vulgar champagne masses a taste of true perfection rarely seen, rarely heard. I was mesmerized by the spectacle, as Lawrence Welk prodded and poked his brilliant captive before the clamoring masses, like an early Christian in the Coliseum, as waiting hungry lions pawed the ground to eat.

I would retreat to the outside garden at night, set a firecracker to a cigarette fuse and look stunned when it exploded as I sat with Thomas and Grandma.

My revenge for Grandma's salad dressing that was not to my taste. In fairness and retrospect my dismay at her curious choice of toppings, may merely have been a creative whim at culinary perfection. One that captured me with the pure velocity of its discord and distaste.

THE SWITCH

My pleasant duty was the daily walking of our English bulldog Sweetie. We were companions and friends. She was to instruct me more perfectly regarding higher principles of character, than the collective series of humans in my early years. She was never overbearing, never devious or pretentious as I discovered freely in the world of humans. She was Sweetie, well-named, an able and true preceptor for a small boy lost in a large and formidable world. We walked back alleys at our leisure, our purposes our own, boy and bulldog, as companions, friends, comrades. Sweetie saw things I did not, trusted humans that I dare not, and so the protector of a young heart that had learned too much, too quickly that the world is an unsafe place for the innocent. Sweetie in those days and perhaps even now, an only true friend and ally. Our walk at its end, I picked up an oddly shaped stick that resembled a bow, because of its unusual curvature. The perfect bow to my arrows, I think.

My tyrant mother confronts our return; "WHAT are you doing with that stick?" I knew but could never betray the direction of this accusation. "It looked like a bow, for my arrows," my sheepish reply resonant with implied guilt. "You were beating that dog, weren't you?" This was not a question, but a statement of fact, it's ludicrous quality approaching spectacle. There is no answer to pure insanity, it is a quality all its own, beyond reason and even hope. Grandma sits on the patio beside her raging daughter but does not speak, the better to observe the unfolding spectacle. "Get a switch, a large one, from this tree. You will see what it feels like to be switched." She has done worse, far worse, than this I think. She switches my bare legs with the passion of her conviction, as I pirouette in small arcs around a tyrant mother's rage and delusion. Grandma watches on unmoved, Sweetie takes swift action in attacking the switch and possible artifacts of hands or legs as presented. Sweetie, locked inside so not to view a punishment richly deserved, punishment that was more painful to her in watching. All as Grandma watches on, silent and unmoving, her daughter in a splendid spectacle of righteous fury. Innocents slain on the field of her battle. My spirit injured more than my body, a profane accusation that I would harm a true friend and protector, now or ever. My life in the twilight world of reasoning as my shame hangs on my soul, for ornament that all might see.

A retrospective of time and years I feel at last, that was one of many smaller retributions for the second burger, a difficult crime long unpunished. But these and the thousand stripes of innocent youth, worn now by the man in a desolation of spirit. Humbled, perhaps broken by masters I cannot defeat, in a race I cannot win. For the indefensible crime I at last can see, the crime of me.

TYRANT

Our tyrant mother deferred immediate punishment for the clear insubordination of the second burger. She would wait in the shadows, her second floor watchtower commanded all fields of view. In the heat of childhood play a week later, I was called before her in her watchtower, the sitting room. This was never good, I awaited a verdict and sentencing for a crime I could not guess.

"Outside just now, you used a word. What word did you use?" My mind a blank, six decades later I still do not recall the word she clearly heard. At ten years of age, my knowledge of bad words was limited and rarely used. Profanity was simply not the language of elementary age kids and it was not mine.

Nonetheless the crime was pronounced, I had escaped punishment for too long, the hangman awaited. Tyrant mother leads me into the bathroom. Will she drown me in the toilet, I wonder. "You are getting your mouth washed out with soap," the sentenced announced. This will be a first for me, I puzzle that it lacks a degree of lethality. I whimper obligingly as she stuffs a bar of soap in my mouth, followed by water. A cakewalk I think, my whimpering increasing for effect. She stands in triumph over me; "Have you learned your lesson?" she commands.

"Yes ma'am," the penitent son. She retreats to her watchtower, I retreat to the yard, just out of view. She must be getting soft, I think, the soap didn't have a bad taste at all.

THE MAGIC DOOR

Our room had a magic door in the corner. It was white, three feet high, two feet wide. There was no handle and it was never opened. We asked what it was, no one knew. This was not a door for adults; it was way too small, beyond their interest or attention. It riveted our interest and our attention. It was a door of mystery, not for adults, so it must be for kids or very small people who lived in a world beyond our sight or imaginings. We watched the door for years, its mystery assumed a life all its own. One day, I don't remember when, Thomas and I decided to open the door; the realization of a mystery.

With no handle and close fitting, opening was challenging, and we could leave no marks on the door that would alert our parents. And it must be reclosed and remain closed. Our secret. The tiny door opened outward to us revealing . . . hanging insulation. This is not the mystery we were waiting to see. But, beyond the insulation lay a perfect small room with steeply canted walls, ceiling. A tiny dormer room, unused, undiscovered, dusty, glorious. A secret clubhouse for kids, unknown to all adults. It was secret, and it was ours. It must remain secret at all cost, no sacrifice too great, no effort too small. A secret to be guarded.

Days went by, followed by weeks, then a hot Oklahoma summer. We met in our secret place, sometimes under the cover of night, sometimes by day, always in secret. Our secret no one would guess, ever. We had candles for light in our tiny dusty room, and cookies,

Kool-Aid and Fig Newtons. We talked at length in whispers what sorts of things we could do here, or bring into this secret place. Nothing obvious, nothing to attract attention.

One hot summer afternoon, our mother called us upstairs to our room. A numbness the color of dread, a clear premonition. She stood in front of our small door, which was standing open. Our hearts sank. This would be bad, very bad.

Three of us regard the offending door. "What is this, in here?" Her face frozen in righteous indignation. "We're not sure." "What's in this jar?" She peers suspiciously at a clear Ball jar half filled with a clear yellow liquid of indeterminate origin. "IS THIS KOOL-AID?" Accusations fly thru the air like bullets, our secret lies wounded and dying at our feet.

The glass of yellow liquid poised precariously for an eternity at our mother's lips. Preparing to prove the ferocity of her accusation, by testing the yellow liquid in her hand. She eyes it with suspicion. Time stops as we await an impossibility. At a last instant, she defects. She never learned that the suspicious yellow liquid in the jar hovering at the edge of her lips was not Kool-Aid. Our secret is saved, forever.

LET THEM EAT CAKE: GERMAN CHOCOLATE CAKE

The cake found an ignoble end in our garbage. I was stunned. A homemade German chocolate cake, three layers high with three types of chocolate frosting, including one laced with coconut. Moist. Taste buds that heretofore had been in long hibernation seemed to awaken, take notice, and riot forth in a celebration. Our mouths seem to sing. Simply put, Thomas and I had never encountered anything so unutterably delicious. Words fail, some things are a matter of pure experience. Such was this cake, residing now in our garbage.

Uneaten for several days, the Oklahoma heat had visited and reduced the priceless culinary masterpiece with spots of mold, like measles. We reflected that our mother somehow preferred to see this culinary triumph in the garbage before she would give it to us. And while we were dismayed, we were not surprised by any actions done by our adoptive mother, or the motives behind them.

And so, in secret, we rescued our beloved cake from its final resting place in the kitchen garbage. Small, round mold spots graced its chocolate flanks on all sides. That's a lot of cake there, easily two, maybe three pounds. A visual feast to two hungry orphans more accustomed to bread, than cake.

I believe the idea hit us at the same time, a flash of pure inspiration that could instantly right this wrong. It went like this: thin slices off the cut, open surface removed any mold there. Careful, selective surgical removal of all remaining spots from frosted areas, returned the cake to a near pristine former glory.

We have achieved whatever our parents could not, by rescuing a true masterpiece. But like so many things of our childhood, it would remain our secret. A secret that perhaps enhanced the enjoyment of this most prized culinary joy. It carried with it the special moment within the heart and minds of two small boys, of not merely saving precious food in what for us was a familiar lifetime career of hunger, but of legitimately saving a true masterpiece, the likes of which remained unparalleled to our experience even now. Their cake was a delight worthy of the gods, and our enjoyment of it was both celebration and reverence of perfection.

The delightful aunt that made this cake did so every summer, "I used ten eggs" she would chant, as a secret to her cake's profound moistness. So each summer, this scene repeated itself again and yet again. Sometimes it was one-third, sometimes one half of the entire German Chocolate Feast, but always, predictably, in the kitchen garbage.

And Thomas and I waited each summer, to rescue this summer's masterpiece. The gods watched on with envy.

THE ESCAPE

We need an escape. An escape beyond an ordinary life of pattern and duty. We escape into movies, music, books, and our dreams of what could be. Thomas and I escaped thru our bedroom window, at night. We waited until all sound in our house ebbed to silence. We waited for sleep to descend, and we were up and mobilized to action. Young child commandos in sneakers, slipping like shadows onto a rusty metal roof leading from our second floor window, to a steeply angled roof. Then, a valley roof, a dormer, along a gutter leading to a five foot stone wall, where we could step off the roof, climb down into the neighbor's yard, and flee under the cover of darkness. The high, dense hedge surrounding our yard hid all movement in the darkness. Commando kids sprinting to the freedom of the neighborhood alleys, where no people walked, no cars drove. Nighttime veiled our movement; all senses alert to any possibility. This was living life on the edge, we breathed in night air, and our spirits rose like smoke in the night. Rose above these darkened alleys, rose above our captive lives. Rose and continued to rise above roofs, trees and neighbor's yards, rose to taste the wild animal joy that sleeps in all the hearts of all creatures. Our hearts were awake here in these dark alleys, and we were free. Our feet moved stealthily in the hard dirt and gravel of the dark alley, our whispers muted. We watched windows, doors, lights, all sound, and any movement in this liquid, languid, living darkness. This night was full of eyes. Our feet catlike, our hearts alive and beating in staccato pulse. We move in this night. This night moves in us. We are the eyes and the living heartbeat of the night. In a world neither kind nor safe, we are, just once, enfolded and safe in her arms. Night gives us her gift of protection, of invisibility against the harsh, corrosive world of daylight. We are safe in this moment, in this place. We are given eyes to see things unseen, and to hear things unheard in this night. A rustle of wind high in the leaves, a heady scent of honeysuckle adrift, the faint flutter, whir of hummingbird moths as they follow the rivers of scent in the night air.

They visit orange trumpet-shaped flowers, pipe vine, that covers the stone walls bordering Jason's house, a pretentiously august home of indeterminate age. It has large, open yards, with graceful plantings. A three car garage with a long concrete drive gives a suitably imposing impression. A foreboding, a shroud of evil seems to hang in the air above this house. Jason Mall is the local bad boy, and Thomas' friend. His father is a dentist with a reputation, a malignant propensity toward mean drunkenness, and beating his son. There is an instant understanding and affinity between us (our mother drinks and beats us, in angry drunken rages). We signal Warner with urgent whispers, and he lets us into his basement. The house is asleep, we move quietly. Jason is almost my brother's age, with olive-skinned good looks and black hair. His is a James Dean kind of coolness, as he tells us his dad beats him with an iron bar. I puzzle how a kid's body can sustain damage with that kind of weapon, which he shrugs off with an indifferent calm. He has learned how to survive his beatings, as we have ours. Jason's dad bellows his name from the top of the stairs, out of our sight. Jason retreats to placate his drunken father. I hear a crashing noise as Jason tumbles backwards down the stairs. It is time to go, before the iron bar is found and used on us. We retreat back into the night, and find a wooded secluded place with a creek. A chorus of frogs provides a welcoming cadence, and fireflies punctuate the darkness, drifting upwind like sparks into the trees. Thomas starts a small campfire, with sticks, and mysteriously produces an entire box of Fig Newtons. He tells me he got the cookies in a store, thru a broken window, the details of which are missing, and patchy.

We gorge on Fig Newtons, and listen to the music of the night, the sights and sounds given only to the two of us. We are the privileged and honored guests to the quiet splendor of night, a symphony of frogs.

These, and other nocturnal adventures are repeated throughout the summer and fall, as we discover our nocturnal freedom from our daytime chains of captivity. We can revisit our lost childhood without the oppression of rules. The thought of punishment, however severe, will wait as we run into the inviting arms of night, of mystery, of adventure. Two young boys drunk with the excitement of sheer possibility. A possibility bound only by the limits of imagination. Our flight is freedom, and our freedom, flight. Our feet sprout wings like Mercury the winged god, and we fly out and upward like smoke thru trees. We circle the yellow orb of moon, and return to our familiar paths and alleys, and finally to our room. Lying in bed panting, dusty sweat still clinging to us, exhausted. We are content and happy. This is the life of a young boy, this. Not our other life of captivity and servitude. Just this. We celebrate the moments given us by a kind Creator, as we are captured by sleep.

Variations of these scenes were repeated many dozens of times throughout several summers. Always undetected, as we worked to perfect our art, the art of escape. We learned stealth, timing, patience, independence. We learned many things that cannot be fully explained or measured, by words. The end of this education was arriving unexpectedly.

On what would be our last adventure thru the window, we both crept back thru our window, and into our bedroom. Waited for our eyes to adjust to the darkness of the room, listened for any tell-tale sound within the house. Silence, but an electric kind of silence, we are jolted in disbelief. Our bedroom door is fully opened. In years, our bedroom door was never open, **never**. Here and now, it yawned before us into a deeper blackness beyond. We await a certain destruction, blinding lights, and barely concealed rage. Punishment above and beyond all we had known.

We waited in the inky darkness, preparing, if possible, for the worst. Nothing. The silence flows seamlessly into the listening malignant darkness. The dread silence speaks volumes. I don't know how long we were frozen there, like salt statues of Sodom and Gomorrah, their fate more preferable to our own. A long passage of time, we whisper," Is their bedroom door open?" Our door met their door in a short hallway. We inch forward, look thru our open door into darkness. Their door, like ours, is never open, ever. It IS open. We are discovered, doomed and beyond help. Our certain destruction awaits us, as we slip into bed. Sleep, merciful sleep, overcomes apprehension. We drift into a yawning dark precipice of dreamless sleep.

The next morning fills quickly with morning routine. We await the pronouncement of our doom. It does not come. No flicker of innuendo, no suggestion of . . . anything. We never knew then, or now, if our parents ever knew of our nighttime adventures. Those adventures came to an abrupt halt though, that night.

An afterthought, I do recall my brother launching himself from another bedroom window two stories up, onto the grass of the neighbor's yard. No roofline to climb down on, just sheer rock wall covered with English Ivy, and Thomas sailing over an asphalt driveway, in a rolling tumble. Unhurt, on grass. He asks if I want to try it, from thirty feet up. I do not. Thomas preens himself. Our grandmother's bedroom window below ours, she never sees her grandson flying thru space to alight on the grass outside her window.

The End.

BATHROOM DUTIES

Rules are strange things, they mark the boundaries of our lives. Talk, don't talk. Get up, sit down. Sleep, eat, don't eat, look, don't look, rules could fill a book, volumes of books. Rules tell us what to do, or not do. They may describe

who we are, or are not.

Thomas and I followed the rules. Some we understood, some we did not. We did not ask why of rule makers, our job was to follow the rules without question. One rule puzzles even now, a lifetime later. I hesitate to mention it, may sound like perversity, and perhaps it is. The rule, you might ask. Bathroom doors remained open, never closed, but this rule was only for Thomas and I. Bath time, potty time, anytime we were inside the bathroom, the door remained open, inviting the interest and attention of the world to our interesting activities within the bathroom.

Our grandmother would shuffle by her bathroom, conveniently located in her bedroom, as we violated her privacy with our clearly visible necessities. For an aging and infirm woman, she would surprise continuously with her stealthy approach, she seemed almost as embarrassed as I. An exercise in mutual humiliation, the child and the senior, neither of us knew why. Rules in a home that did not belong to her or myself. A rule devised to strip the small dignity from a small child, it was effective in doing just that. Its purpose a mystery. A first in my very young life, the denial of simple privacy for the purpose of simple relief. A punishment unto itself. The occasional visitors to our home invited to the viewing, if accidental. Uncle E. K., walking in unconsciously humming a tune as I lay sprawled in the bathtub. A stumbled apology, his kindness still remembered. He honored our privacy if our parents refused to. Beyond our humiliation, perfectly done with a daily dividend, we could not guess the purpose of this rule. But it was a violation of the spirit, the denial of simple modesty, they seemed intent on stripping our souls to bedrock.

In our homeless days we were permitted privacy, here in our home we were denied. If I am awkward in telling this awkward tale, it is in the defense of the honor of children. Long after being a child, I have come to know that children are very special, perhaps the most special of all. Their innocence and trust a pure treasure. A wealth uniquely theirs, our lost selves, the people we were before we were old, tired, and worn down by a lifetime of rules. Children themselves, the treasure that I never was. Their safety, security our sacred duty, their happiness and joy, our reward. Their laughter a ray from heaven. In the spirit of kindness, a suggestion that doors be opened for children, that their imagination and spirit can find wings; doors closed that we may hold and protect the perfect treasure that is a child. Until the time that we turn to marvel that the living treasure we held in the secret door of the heart, has now grown wings of pure magnificence, as a winged glory from a chrysalis. And the perfect wonder as the glory takes flight, as we watch, the doors flung wide open at last. And we behold beauty, grown from love, and from beauty, love.

VISITING A CHILD

I think in mysterious ways, adults are hardwired to children. Plugged directly into the other's limbic system, as it were. A child, anyone's child, smiles at you, the sun is suddenly shining. Children's laughter, like a sudden message from Heaven. Their tears, the world becomes a broken place, beyond any hope of repair.

From the height and perspective of advancing years, I visit the child I was. Thinking to cast light in a place of considerable darkness. Thinking to console a child lost and adrift on the ocean of life, my own life. The child is two years old; his parents, his family, his home is lost to him.

His innocence sacrificed on the altar of chaos. I will sit down with the child I was, cross legged on the ground, so that I can look into his eyes, which are brown and soft, like a fawn's eyes. There is innocence there, pure, simple, sweet like a hidden aroma of honeysuckle flowers carried on the night air. This child, he is the perfect being that I have never been. Yet there is frailty and fragility there in this small being that is beyond my grasp and understanding. This road before him is too long, too wide, and too endless. His small legs are those of a toddler, the distance is too great for an adult; how can this very small child manage so vast a distance. Alone.

As any parent, I wonder this and a thousand things such, all in a moment. I am crushed under the weight of questions, all that I cannot answer, looking into the eyes of the child I was. There is something here that is far beyond pain, something elemental and simple like the child I sit here with. I could tell him to hope, but does he know what hope is, he can barely walk. Perhaps I can tell him that I will be waiting for him at the end of his very long road. Perhaps a hug to his frail body, a suggestion of affection, tenderness, and love that has escaped us both. A promise then. A promise that I will wait for him with arms outstretched at the end of his impossibly long journey, on his impossibly frail legs.

He should not see my tears, but my heart lies broken in the dust for this child. His pain and fear I cannot assuage. For all the things I would offer, to give him comfort now, if only I could. This will be a short visit today, with this child I once was. His innocence is too great, my wisdom too lean and gaunt, ravaged by years and time.

We will visit again, soon I hope. But for now I need to leave, to escape back thru the years and time, to the one I have become. The pain has become too great in this ancient heart, and there is still a distance to go, on aged but stronger legs.

The promise holds now and always. I will wait for this child however long the road, and tortuous the path. I hope to visit him from time to time, tell him I am here. He thinks he is alone. If God has angels, I ask he be given his very own that protects, guides, helps him. And above all, loves him, as he seems to have missed that here on earth.

We will visit again. Soon I hope. And the promise now and always, I will wait for him, with arms open wide, at the end of his very long road.

EPILOGUE: A POSTSCRIPT I

No story of a childhood complete without parents. The most difficult part of this story, is this part. I had been putting it off, but it is inseparable, it draws, pulls all other details of our childhood into it, like a black hole. And like a black hole, no light escapes. It was a dangerous place, I wonder that we survived it, I continue to wonder if we have survived it.

As orphans, we were wards of the state. The state, its domestic arm, struggled to find adoptive homes for its many orphans, and in those times, there were many of us. It was post World War II, the great war that consumed millions of lives and untold suffering. Vast production of guns, tanks, ships and bombers no longer needed, a working class languished in poverty. The Baby Boom, we were the unique product of a post war time. For many like us, it was a time of abject poverty.

These were our beginnings, Thomas and I, from such a time and place. From years in orphanages and foster homes, Thomas and I were introduced to our forever adoptive parents, Norman and Sadie, at ages four and six. On paper, they were ideal parents, both college graduates. They made money, had resources they could provide. They drove a new car. They looked like an ordinary couple, a world of possibility at their feet. They were young, not yet the monsters they would become.

As we were discovering our new home, they were discovering alcohol. Red Smirnoff, to be exact, eighty proof, intemperate amounts. I remember early rides to neighboring Arkansas where they would buy a case of vodka. My brother and I were given pink and white snowballs, we fought passionately over the pink snowball. Our snowball wars.

The seeds planted, an evil grew, engulfing all of our lives in its tendrils. Evenings were to become dangerous times, our mother an angry drunk. Her violent rages vented on Thomas or myself, in the pantry, a solitary place. Her anger splendid and fiery, we were the unwitting focus, and the catalyst of her rage, planted in fertile ground. A mercy she did not find sterner implements than hands, blows falling on us from all quarters, fueled by a bottomless pit of hatred and fury. Smirnoff the catalyst that fueled her fire, her change agent.

Perhaps their expectation that their adoptive children would give them the love they seemed to lack, in their joyless marriage. Love a fragile flower, it did not bloom in our house. What did bloom was something evil, something that felt like tangible malice and it was watching Thomas and me.

It was a species of horror, living and purposeful, that came to live with us in our childhood home. A quality of fear, terror and uncertainty was the weather and the forecast, we sailed our small boats in treacherous waters that might overwhelm us at any moment. We came to be uncertain if we would survive this place, our new home. Our bodies did survive, if our souls did not, we were victims of a private holocaust, its intent no less evil, if on a lesser scale. On the surface, we were a respectable family and appearances would be maintained. Breaking that mold, we became runaways, small fugitives from a punishing time and place.

I do not recall our father speaking much, and then in softened abbreviated words that seemed meaningless. Father - son, simple conversations rarely occurred, our mother would handle those grimmer duties.

A small aluminum boat and motor, our father fancied himself a fisherman. The launching of this small boat testing the limits of my father's abilities, we would find ourselves on a quiet part of a glassy lake. Lures did not invite fish, I cannot recall any effort of any fish, ever, attempting our capture. I wondered if there were any fish in that lake, repeated fishing trips futile, always. Nor did our father invite conversations that may ruin our fishing chances that were already ruined. I puzzled why we went on these joyless trips, a purpose here I could not fathom. I did not know then, that our father was fishing for me, his youngest son. The fishing expeditions that at first seemed pointless would steer toward deeper more dangerous waters. The catch would be the innocence of children. As children we knew little, but this did not feel like love, or like a home. There was stench and a foul odor, as when hope and dreams are left crushed and dying from intemperate and uncaring trampling. Young souls blasted by evil, our childhood roots and dreams lay in rocky, barren ground. Thomas and I survived, our innocence did not.

Our father, never healthy, would incur a stroke that would kill him. Our mother weary of caring for her new burden, she invited, encouraged his demise.

Though he could not speak or walk, he was lucid. He would accommodate her wish, she would continue her solitary life alone. I wonder that she grieved his passing.

My last visit with our adoptive father was brief and memorable. He was failing, this would be a goodbye visit. His expression contrite, never before seen, monosyllables trickled from his lips, unintelligible. He's trying to tell me he's sorry, downcast eyes convey a rare message. Our lovely Aunt Euvea honks the car horn, we will miss our flight. I see my father here, dying at last, his apology for our childhood innocence destroyed, on lips that cannot speak. The message received, Thomas and Euvea anxious to leave this place, we will be carried away in flight. This is a gift he gives himself, his wordless apology for the death of innocence. Perhaps his soul would not allow him to journey further into his death, without a final accounting, in a wordless but heartfelt apology. His apology received, it is time to leave. Flight awaits. Kindness eludes me, even now. Forgiveness, a divine gift not given to me, not yet. I have flown through these years and this life, his wordless apology a fragile memory that I cultivate in the fertile, deep earth, with a wordless, reluctant hope, that it may one day, bloom as mercy.

EPILOGUE II

Anger lived there, in the deepest reaches of the heart. Burning long and low, I would warm my hands against a winter chill, it gave off a heat and fire all its own. A suggestion of nobility, like a prince bereft of his birthright. Heathcliffe, a smoldering passion, never realized. In anger, a constancy that the world lacked, a kind of fidelity that never rejected, but always embraced me, we became the most intimate of friends. It found me in darkness, breathed life into a soul that became indifferent to life, to living.

My friend, companion, at times my master, I would pause to consider its steady, long life in the deep regions of heart. Was there an injury, a hurt long forgotten that welcomed this interesting guest, that came to visit, yet now lived in a place I considered to be home. I look more carefully, I consider signs and symptoms of malady perhaps, an underlying disease, an immune response protecting me, perhaps from a greater unknown evil. In classical times, disease lived in 'vapors' unseen, invisible, I hearken to classical times, following a distant thread, looking for a beginning.

The answer suddenly clear, I see it before me. My anger at God. The God of our fathers, the God that hung the cosmos as endless beauty and mystery, the God of my own being, my anger rages from primitive times, in unseen secret places. My own Father, who watched me running on three year old legs, with breathless speed, and smiled well-pleased at a beautiful child, His very own. His smile warmed me, an orphan, His smile was my home. The place I would live. Years passed, time sped by in a vanishing flood, this anger as a seed, now rooted deeply into heart tissue, the very connection of soul, and matter to spirit. A fire and anger against God. I see the reason, this guest that claims my home. It is pain but not just pain, a pure angst, a heart torn from its moorings. A living child lost in the world, a true orphan, that is, at last, given a family, but a family of beasts. A family of true carnivores that dine on the flesh on innocence. They are hungry, these beasts given to me as family, their teeth tear my body, heart, soul; they are hungry and angry. I cannot defend, my shield of innocence, devoured. I live in dark places, night surrounds me; I am more lost now than I have ever been. I construct walls to shield and protect me even as they are destroyed. I will be devoured slowly, watching my demise as I am eaten alive. Terror and fear my companions, anger the mortar of these high walls that I must build as quickly as they are broken and eaten by beasts. Anger my defense, to a God who has rescued a small orphan, only to deliver it to beasts that only resemble parents, they are not real humans. Their anger and malice to me, fiery and spectacular, beyond my imagining. I cling to the wreckage of my small ship, I am adrift in violent storms in a deep ocean. I will drown here, or be eaten by the beasts that live in these deep waters. Jaws that reach for me, tentacles that pull me into the depths, I am lost, forgotten, and alone. It is night, I am adrift in deep water, I wonder at the Father who smiled once, has brought me here to this place, where wild animals live. I am mere flesh for their hunger, I am not a human or a child. God does not smile or I cannot see His smile in this darkness. He does not live in places like this, yet He has sent me here, an orphan child. My anger rescues me from drowning in deep waters in a dark night, I build my walls, my shield against these hungry beasts, my wall and shield is anger itself, it will protect me, save me. There is nothing else here that will save a child.

Years flown by, become a lifetime, I consider this rage and anger at God that He has brought me here to this twilight. My childhood gone, and with it the violent storms that threatened. Time has led me to this high place, above the flood, the beasts that haunted me now dead and gone, mere memory. A dream perhaps. A green forest in springtime now around me, a setting sun enamels clouds in gold brilliance. A rising wind in rustling leaves, in a quiet place, a rare sunset before me as a feast. My spirit composed, I awaken to see life all about me, my broken ship washed up on the shores of beauty. The thousand lashes given to me then a child and now, His perfect gift to me, as this setting sun before me on this high mountain, in springtime, a rustle of wind in the leaves. He has brought me here, at last. I am finishing this story now, as wind and rain pass over. I pause to consider this ending, I see a rainbow over the distant mountain. I know it as a word and a promise, His comment on my story. Who else can speak so?

The story no longer my own, about me. The burden laid down. This is His story, His excellent work, and about Him, after all.

CPSIA information can be obtained
at www.ICGtesting.com
Printed in the USA
FSHW021938180719